THE BASIC SCIENCE EDUCATION SERIES

Saving Our Wildlife

by BERTHA MORRIS PARKER

LABORATORY SCHOOLS, UNIVERSITY OF CHICAGO

Checked for Scientific Accuracy by

GLADYS K. McCOSH

Professor of Zoölogy, Wellesley College

COVER PHOTOGRAPH
FLORIDA STATE NEWS BUREAU,
TALLAHASSEE

6

California State Series. Published by CALIFORNIA
STATE DEPARTMENT OF EDUCATION.
Sacramento, 1959

Saving Our Wildlife

A Bird You Will Never See

IN THE days of your great-great-great-great-grandfathers and your great-great-great-great-grandmothers there were no automobiles or airplanes. There were no television sets or radios. But your great-great-great-great-grandfathers and your great-great-great-great-grandmothers probably saw something that you will never be able to see. They probably saw huge flocks of passenger pigeons.

A hundred and fifty years ago there were billions of passenger pigeons. Seventy-five years ago there were still millions of them. Now there are none at all. The last passenger pigeon anyone knows about died September 1, 1914. This pigeon was in a zoo in Cincinnati, Ohio. It had lived all its life in the zoo.

You can see from the picture on page 2 that passenger pigeons were beautiful birds. On page 28 there is a picture of a pair of mourning doves. From the two pictures you can tell that passenger pigeons looked very much like mourning doves. But they were larger. They grew to be about a foot and a half long.

Passenger pigeons lived in flocks. They flew south in the fall in flocks, too. While there were still many of them, they flew south in such crowds that the noise their wings made could be heard a long way off. Sometimes so many of them roosted in a tree that big branches of the tree were broken off. The great flocks of pigeons were one of the wonders of the bird world.

3

Passenger pigeons ate acorns, beechnuts, and many other kinds of seeds. They ate berries. They also ate some insects. They were big eaters. Often they made a nuisance of themselves by flying down to a farmer's field and eating wheat and corn he had just planted.

What happened to all the passenger pigeons? Why aren't there any now?

Cutting down our forests had a great deal to do with making the passenger pigeon disappear. The pigeons got most of their food from forest trees. They needed thick forests for nesting places, too. When many of our forests were cut down, it was harder for the pigeons to find homes.

But the guns and nets of hunters were even more important than tree-cutting in making the passenger pigeon disappear. Passenger pigeons were good to eat. Besides, they were easy to shoot or catch. As many as fifty nests could often be found in one tree. Young birds brought higher prices than older birds. By coming to a nesting place, hunters could catch hundreds of dollars' worth of young pigeons in a few days.

The hunters killed enormous numbers of passenger pigeons. Sometimes they even shot them just for fun. There were so many that people did not think it would make any difference how many the hunters killed.

But it did make a difference. After a while there were millions of pigeons instead of billions. Then there were thousands instead of millions. Finally there were only a few. They were scarce enough to be put in zoos.

When people saw that the passenger pigeon was disappearing, they passed laws to keep hunters from killing it. But the laws came too late. The passenger pigeon was soon gone. There is no way of getting it back again.

The American Bison

The story of the American bison is much like the one you just read. But it has a happier ending.

American bison are not true buffaloes. Most of us, however, call them buffaloes.

When white men first came to America, there were millions of buffaloes here. Some lived east of the Mississippi River. But they were much more common on the grassy plains of the West.

The Indians killed many buffaloes. They ate buffalo meat. They used the hides for clothes and wigwams.

The buffaloes, however, were able to hold their own against the Indians. When the white settlers began to move west, there were still millions of buffaloes. They lived in great herds. Sometimes some of the buffaloes of a herd would be startled and would begin to run. The whole herd would follow. There would be a buffalo stampede. It was very dangerous to be in the way of a stampede of these big animals.

5

White men began shooting buffaloes. They killed many to get meat, just as the Indians had. They wanted the hides, too. Buffalo robes—skins with the long hair still on them—were very common. The early settlers shot many buffaloes because they were afraid of stampedes. They shot some just for the fun of hunting.

There were so many buffaloes that no one thought that they could ever all be killed. But more and more people moved west. They shot more and more buffaloes. The buffaloes disappeared from east of the Mississippi. There were still, however, enormous herds left on the grassy plains of the West.

The killing of buffaloes went on faster and faster. Besides, the settlers began plowing up the western plains. Plowing up these plains took away food and homes from the buffaloes. The great herds grew smaller. Buffaloes at last became scarce.

But there were still some. A few people set to work to keep these from being killed off. Places were set aside where they could live safely.

This time something was done before it was too late. The small herds in the places set aside for them got along well. They have grown larger. In all the herds put together there are now several thousand buffaloes.

Lake Sturgeon

Too Much Killing

The stories of the passenger pigeon and the buffalo are both stories of too much killing. Many others like them could be told. We do not have nearly so many wild animals as we once had, and too much killing is a large part of the reason why.

Six *F*'s explain most of the killing of our birds and other wild animals. The six *F*'s are *food, fur, feathers, fun, fear,* and *fuel.*

The great auk is another bird you will never see. The last one died about a hundred years ago. This large bird was killed chiefly for food.

From its picture on page 9 you can tell that the great auk looked very much like a penguin. Its flipper-like wings were small and weak. Like the penguin, it could swim very well, but it could not fly.

The auks nested in great numbers on a few small islands on the eastern shores of North America. Fishermen found these islands. At nesting time it was easy to kill the auks. Sometimes the birds were eaten at once. Sometimes the meat was salted and stored for the winter. Hundreds of boatloads of auks were carried away from the islands each year. Thousands of eggs were gathered and eaten, too. No wonder the great auk disappeared!

Many, many other kinds of animals have been killed for food. The lake sturgeon is one of them. This big fish was killed chiefly for its eggs. Not many people liked to eat the fish itself. The eggs were not taken from the water after they were laid; the fish were caught and the eggs were taken from their bodies. The lake sturgeon was once very common. There are still some left, but not many.

Marten

Many of our wild animals have soft, beautiful fur. We have killed them for their fur. The marten is one of our fur-bearers. This shy little animal lives in deep forests. It used to be common. Now it is scarce. Unless we are careful, the marten and many of our other fur-bearers will soon be gone.

The snowy egret is a bird of our southern coastlands. It has beautiful white feathers—so beautiful that women used to use them in great numbers as hat trimming. Early in the 1900's so many egrets were being killed for their feathers that the bird was about to disappear. But laws against killing it were passed in time. Snowy egrets are again fairly common.

Some birds have been killed for their feathers even though their feathers were not pretty. The great auk was killed chiefly for food, but thousands were killed to get feathers for featherbeds.

Sometimes men kill animals just for fun. You may have heard people talk about the fun of going hunting. It is fun to be able to shoot a gun well, just as it is fun to be able to play any game well. But hunting is not fun for the animals that are hunted. Besides, we have to stop to think whether we can afford to let our wild animals be killed just for fun.

Hunters have shot many duck hawks for fun. And duck hawks have helped hunters have fun in another way. They can be trained to hunt small animals such as rabbits. Using hawks to help hunt is called "falconry." Hunters rob the nests of the duck hawks to get young birds to train. Besides, some people steal duck hawk eggs just for the fun of putting them in their collections of bird eggs. In these ways the duck hawk has almost been killed off.

The big bear on the inside covers is a grizzly. Grizzly bears are large, powerful animals. There are not many now. Men killed them because they were afraid of them. Grizzly bears sometimes caught sheep and other animals that men raised. Men shot grizzlies to protect themselves and their tame animals.

It probably seems queer to think of killing animals for fuel, but some have been killed for that reason. Men killed whales, for example, to get their oil. In the early days of our country, whale oil was an important fuel, especially for lamps.

We do not need whale oil for fuel now. But we have found many other uses for the oil, and whaling still goes on. If we do not stop killing our whales, some kinds will soon be gone.

9

Great Auk

Duck Hawk

Fewer Forest Homes

Too much killing is not the whole story of why we do not have so many wild animals as we used to have. Taking away their homes is another important part of the story. You have already found out that taking away its homes helped make the passenger pigeon disappear. It helped do away with the great herds of buffalo.

All animals have to have places to live, just as we do. Different kinds of animals need different kinds of homes.

The passenger pigeon, you remember, lived in forests. Many animals have forest homes. As we have cut down our forests, we have made it harder and harder for these animals to find places to live. We have made it harder for them to get food, too, for most animals that live in forests get food from the forests.

It is not easy for us to picture how many trees we have cut down since white men first came to our country. The early settlers cut down many trees to make room for their houses. They used the logs to build their houses. They cut down many more trees so that they could plant crops on the land where the trees had been. They cut down millions of trees.

10

Ivory-billed Woodpecker

Prairie Dog

Probably the early settlers who cleared the land to make homes for themselves did not stop to think that they were taking away the homes of wild animals. But that is just what they were doing.

Forest fires have taken away the homes of wild animals, too. People are to blame for many of the forest fires we have had.

The ivory-billed woodpecker is disappearing partly because it has lost many of its forest homes. This woodpecker lives in swampy forests where there are large trees. There are fewer forests of this kind than there used to be. And there are so few ivory-billed woodpeckers left that people who are trying to save them keep the homes of these birds a secret. If these woodpeckers should be bothered by hunters now, they would soon all be gone. In fact, by the time you read this book there may be no "ivory-bills."

The bobcat is another animal that needs a forest home. If the forests where it can live disappear, it will disappear, too. The bobcat is a meat-eater. Many of the small animals it catches live in the forest. Cutting down the forests where the bobcat lives would take away its homes and much of its food.

Bobcat

The moose also lives in forests. Moose eat plants. In the winter they eat twigs of trees and bushes. In the summer they eat mostly plants that grow in shallow lakes and slow-moving streams. Moose are not nearly so common as they used to be. Hunters have killed too many. Besides, many of their forest homes have been taken away from them.

Men are still cutting down trees. We need the wood for building houses. We need it, too, for making such things as furniture and paper.

To save the wild animals of our forests, we do not have to stop all tree-cutting. Some trees can be cut out of a forest without taking away the homes of the forest animals. Most animals get along best in forests that are not too thick. Moose, for example, cannot live in thick woods. They need woods in which there are open spaces—spaces where enough sunshine can reach the ground to make bushes grow. But the cutting down of trees should always be planned by people who understand what kinds of homes forest animals need.

Moose

Fewer Grass-Land Homes

Our grass-lands were once a wonderful place for wild animals. The plants that grew there furnished food for many kinds of animals. As you already know, there were millions of buffaloes in the grass-lands. There were also millions of deer and of pronghorns like those in the picture on page 31. There were even more millions of small animals.

The prairie dog is one of the small animals that lived in the grass-lands in enormous numbers. The lower picture on page 10 shows this little animal.

Prairie dogs live in burrows in the ground. They pile up soil around the entrances to their burrows. They live in big groups. In the days of the early settlers there were prairie dog "towns" that covered many acres. There were even some that covered many square miles. In a very large "town" there might be several hundred million prairie dogs.

The prairie chicken is one of the birds that used to be very common in the grass-lands. Its picture is on page 15. The prairie chicken builds its nest on the ground. The tall grass around the nest hides it.

When white men moved into the grass-lands, they took away the homes of millions of prairie dogs and prairie chickens, just as they took away the homes of millions of buffaloes. They crowded many other animals of the grass-lands out of some of their homes, too.

The settlers turned much of the prairie into farms. It was easy to turn this land into farms. There were no trees to be cut down.

The settlers did not plow up all the grass-lands. They used some for grazing land. They brought sheep and cattle to graze on this land.

Just as in cutting down the forests, people did not realize that they were taking away the homes of millions of wild animals. There are still prairie dogs, but there are not nearly so many big towns as there once were. There are still prairie chickens, but it has been many years since they were common.

Many grass-land animals were killed at the same time that their homes were being taken away from them. When there was no longer so much grass to hide in, the animals were easy targets for hunters.

In the end the people who moved to the grass-lands spoiled large areas even for themselves. They put too many sheep and cattle on some of the grazing lands. The sheep and cattle ate the land bare. The plowed fields were covered with crops which did not hold the soil in place so well as the prairie grasses had. There is not much rain in many parts of the grass-lands, and the soil is dry. After a while the farmers noticed that the soil was not so deep as it had been. Some of it was blowing away. Some was being washed away by rains, too.

Perhaps you have seen pictures of great dust storms in our grass-land country. These storms happened because too much of the soil was uncovered. It was so light and dry that the wind could blow it away.

In places so much soil has now been carried away that no plants will grow there. Of course, no wild animals can live there either. People have had to move away from these places, too.

Soil is very important for all kinds of wildlife. Most land plants have to have soil. Animals cannot live without plants. Saving our soil is one very important part of saving our wildlife. We have not saved the soil of our grass-lands very well.

Fewer Water Homes

To get more land for farms, the people of our country have drained many marshes. Draining marshes has made nearby ponds and small lakes dry up. Fewer marshes and ponds and lakes have meant fewer homes for our water animals.

The whooping crane is one of the water birds that have had many of their homes taken away from them. This crane is a marsh bird. Its nest is a little island made out of marsh grass and reeds. It gets much of its food from the water.

The "whooper" lives in marshes in grass-lands. It is almost as tall as a man. Its spread-out wings measure seven feet. Because it lives in open country and because it is so big, it made an easy target for hunters. Now it has almost disappeared. Too many were killed, and too many of its homes were taken away. No nests have been found in our country for many years. But every year a few whoopers still come from Canada to spend the winter in our South.

The white pelican is another water bird that has lost many of its homes. It builds its nests on the ground near a pond or lake. Often it chooses a sandy island. The pelican eats fish.

15

Prairie Chicken

Whooping Crane

It catches them in a pouch that hangs from its lower bill. You can see the pouch in the picture on page 17.

Once nests of the white pelican could be found in many parts of our country. Now there are no nests east of North Dakota. All the white pelicans would now be gone if places for them to live had not been set aside.

Birds are not the only animals that have lost their homes when wet lands were drained. Of course, many frogs and fish have. Many little furry animals such as muskrats have, too.

Draining wet lands is only one of the ways we have taken homes away from our water animals. In many places we have left the water but have made it unfit for animals. We have, for instance, spoiled many of our lakes and streams for fish.

We have dumped waste materials from factories into some lakes and streams. These waste materials may kill the fish. At any rate, they are likely to kill the plants in the water, and if there are no plants, the fish will not have the food they need. They all live on plants or on other animals that eat plants.

Pacific Salmon

White Pelican

Too much mud in water makes it a bad home for fish, just as waste materials from factories do. Running water almost always carries some soil. But before our forests were cut down, our rivers did not usually carry enough soil to make them muddy. Tree roots help hold soil in place. Cutting down the forests let the rains wash soil into the rivers much faster.

Plowing the land made our rivers muddier, too. Rains can easily wash loose soil away. Now some of our rivers are too muddy for many of the fishes that once lived in them.

The homes of some fish have been disturbed in still another way. The picture on page 16 shows one of the fishes whose homes we have disturbed.

Salmon of this kind live most of their lives in the Pacific Ocean. But they both begin and end their lives in rivers. When it is time to lay their eggs, the salmon swim for miles up rivers that flow into the Pacific. They often have to jump up falls on the way. They lay their eggs in the rivers and then die. The young salmon that hatch from the eggs live in the rivers for a while. Then they swim down to the sea.

17

Mule Deer

The Columbia is one of the rivers up which the salmon swim. Not long ago a big dam was built across the Columbia. The water falling over the dam drives the machines in a big electric power plant.

The dam would have kept the salmon from swimming up and down the river. To help the fish get past the dam, fish ladders were built.

Of course, fish ladders are not ladders of the kind we use. Can you imagine a fish climbing a real ladder? A fish ladder is a line of small pools. Each pool is a little higher than the one before it. The salmon can jump easily from one pool to the next. The old salmon can still go up the river to lay their eggs, and the young salmon can still swim down to the sea.

Other fishes besides salmon have had their homes taken away by the building of dams. Fish ladders help some of them, too. Not all dams, however, have fish ladders to let fish get around them.

Draining wet lands has given us more land for farming. Building dams across rivers has given us more electric power. But we may decide that we have paid too much for this land and this power when we think of the animals whose homes we have taken away.

A Mistaken Idea

Not long ago people were trying to save the mule deer in one of our western forests. They decided that, since mountain lions eat mule deer, a good way to help the deer would be to kill all the mountain lions. They began killing the lions. Soon there was not one left in the region.

At first the plan worked just as it was supposed to. In a few years there were thousands of deer.

But the forest was not big enough for so many deer. They could not find enough to eat. In the winter many of them starved to death. The ones that lived ate every leaf and twig and piece of bark that they could find. They killed many of the forest trees and bushes. In the end some of the deer had to be shot.

The wild animals which men hunt for food are called *game animals*. Meat-eaters like the mountain lion are called *animals of prey*. The idea that the best way to save the deer was to kill all the mountain lions turned out to be a mistaken idea. In many other cases, too, the idea that the best way to save our game animals is to kill our animals of prey has turned out to be wrong.

Mountain Lion

Coyote

When people leave a region alone, the number of wild plants and animals in it stays about the same year after year. There is a kind of balance among all the living things in the region.

Before people had anything to do with the forest you were told about, the number of plants and deer and mountain lions stayed about the same. The mountain lions kept the number of deer from growing larger. And the deer ate about the same number of plants each year. Killing off the mountain lions upset this balance.

"But," hunters say, "the story of the mule deer and the mountain lion was an unusual case. No hunters were allowed to shoot any of the deer in the forest. In places where hunting is allowed, there would be ever so much more game for us to shoot if the animals of prey were killed."

Really it is not fair to blame our meat-eaters for the scarcity of our game animals. They do kill some, but men kill ever and ever so many more. Before hunters began killing passenger pigeons, there were enormous flocks of these birds in spite of all the wild animals that ate them. And in spite of the mountain lions, there used to be millions of deer.

Our meat-eaters are a real help to hunters in one way. A meat-eater catches the animal that is easiest to catch. Often this animal is weak or sick. By taking out the weak and sick animals, the meat-eaters help keep the flocks and herds of game in good shape. They help keep diseases from spreading.

Farmers often agree with hunters that animals of prey should be killed. They want them killed because animals of prey sometimes kill cattle, sheep, and other tame animals.

It is true that animals of prey do kill some tame animals. But farmers often blame them for much more harm than they really do.

In the western part of our country the coyote is one of our common animals of prey. Farmers blame the coyote for doing a great deal of harm. A glimpse of a coyote is a signal to a farmer to get his gun.

But it has been found that coyotes are often blamed for harm they have not done. A thousand cattle were found dead on a ranch in the Southwest. Their dead bodies showed that coyotes had been having a feast. "How terrible for coyotes to kill a thousand cattle," people said. But later it was found that the coyotes had not killed the cattle. The cattle had died because dry weather had killed the grass. Stories like this could be told of other animals of prey.

The animals of prey that farmers kill are often helping the farmers. Jack rabbits eat crops. The same coyote that once in a while catches a sheep kills many jack rabbits. In the same way, the hawk that sometimes catches a chicken also catches rats and mice and insects that harm the farmer's crops.

Do you see, then, that it would not be a good plan to kill off all our animals of prey?

An S O S for Our Wild Plants

Plants are a part of our wildlife, just as animals are. And we have treated our wild plants as badly as we have treated our wild animals.

Plowing up the grass-lands took away the homes of many wild animals. It took away the homes of many wild plants, too. The chief plants of the grass-lands, of course, are grasses, but many beautiful wild flowers grow with the grasses.

Cutting down our forests ruined the homes of many forest animals. It also ruined the homes of many wild flowers. Many of our wild flowers will not grow except in woods. It goes without saying that cutting down the forests meant the killing of millions and millions of trees.

Not many trees like the one in the picture on this page are left. The name beside the picture tells you that the tree is a Sequoia redwood.

Sequoia redwoods are often called "Big Trees." They certainly are big. Some of them grow to be more than 300 feet tall. The trunks may be more than 25 feet across.

Some Big Trees are very, very old, too. Probably you know that the age of a tree can be told by the rings in the wood of its trunk. One Big Tree

22

Sequoia Redwood

that was cut down was found to be 3,126 years old. Some of the Big Trees that are still alive are thought to be even older. They are among the oldest living things on earth. The "General Sherman," one of the Big Trees alive now, is believed to be about 4,000 years old. It was, we think, some 3,500 years old when Columbus discovered America.

Of course, one of these giants has a great deal of wood in it. Men cut them down and sold the wood. They had cut down a great many before anyone thought about saving them.

But at last people saw that unless something was done the Big Trees would soon be gone. They began to try to save them. Saving them was not easy. While some people wanted to save them, others still wanted to cut them down for their wood. No wonder, when one tree would give enough lumber to build a whole town!

Today most of the groves of Big Trees are safe inside three national parks. These parks are in California because that is the only place in the world where these giant trees grow.

There are still some Sequoia redwoods outside parks, and some of them are being cut down. But at least we have saved some of our Big Trees.

The Sequoia redwood is not the only tree that has become scarce. There are many others. The coast redwood, a cousin of the Sequoia redwood, is one of them. The beautiful white pine is another.

Dogwood

Today our government owns a great deal of our forest land. It is trying to save our trees. But much of our best forest land is still owned by people who are cutting down the trees of the forests as fast as they can. Too many trees are still being cut down.

Fires are still turning forests into tree graveyards. Some forest fires are started by lightning. But many more are started by people who are careless about using fire. Campers forget to put out their campfires. Sparks fall into piles of dry leaves. The leaves flame up. Soon many trees are blazing. Or careless smokers toss lighted matches or cigarettes into dry leaves.

We have taken away the homes of many wild flowers. Besides, we have almost killed out the wild flowers in some of the places which are left for them to live in. We have almost killed them out by picking too many.

Perhaps you wonder why picking wild flowers does any harm. You do not kill a plant just by picking its flowers. But flowers make seeds. If all the flowers are picked from a plant, it cannot make any seeds to start new plants.

To get its flowers, people sometimes pull up a whole plant. Sometimes, too, they dig up plants to take home to their gardens. Some wild plants will grow in our gardens, but many will not.

The flowering dogwood is a small tree. It is much scarcer than it once was. It grows in open woods in the shade of larger trees, and many of its homes have been taken away. Besides, many dogwood trees have been killed by having their branches stripped off.

The black-eyed Susan is a grass-land flower. It lost many of its homes when the grass-lands were plowed up. But it has helped save itself by spreading to the meadows in the eastern part of our country.

Of all our beautiful wild flowers one of those that is most likely to disappear is the showy ladyslipper. The showy ladyslipper is an orchid.

You may have seen orchids in flower shops. Most orchids sold there are raised in greenhouses or are brought from warmer countries. But there are some orchids that grow wild in our country. The showy ladyslipper is one of them.

A great many ladyslippers used to grow wild in our woods. But people picked too many. They dug up too many to take home to their gardens.

These orchids have to have a certain kind of soil. The soil in most gardens is not right for them. Besides, it is very hard to dig them up without hurting their roots.

In greenhouses some kinds of orchids are raised from seed. But no one has ever been able to raise a showy ladyslipper from seed.

There are almost no showy ladyslippers left. If you ever find one of these flowers growing in the woods, look at it, but do not pick it. You surely want to help keep this beautiful flower from dying out.

There are many other wild flowers that are growing scarce. Unless we answer their S O S for help, they may disappear.

25

Showy Ladyslipper

Black-eyed Susan

Why Save Our Wildlife?

What difference does it make if we do kill off many kinds of wild plants and animals? Why should we try to save our wildlife?

Probably these questions seem very foolish to you. But many people ask them.

Some of our wild plants and animals are very useful. They have helped make our country rich. We should try to save them so that they will keep on giving us things we need.

If we cut down too many trees, after a while there will be no trees left to furnish us with wood. If we catch too many fish, some day there will be no more fish for us to catch. If we kill too many furry animals, in time all our fur-bearers will be gone.

One of the reasons why we have to think a great deal about saving our wildlife is that the people who settled our country did not think about it at all. There were so many trees and so many wild animals that no

Beaver

one believed that they could ever all be used. People were very wasteful. Hunters, for instance, often killed buffaloes just to get the tongues for food.

Now we see our wildlife disappearing. It is important for us to do something. We do not want our grandchildren to have too many stories to tell like the one about the passenger pigeon.

Even if our wild animals and plants did not furnish us with food, fur, wood, and other useful things, we should save them because they help make our country beautiful and interesting. People travel thousands of miles to see our groves of Big Trees. In our national parks crowds of people watch the animals. It is fun to have a pair of robins nest in your own back yard. And how much we would miss our wild flowers if they disappeared!

Another reason we should save our wildlife is that killing off one kind of plant or animal upsets the balance in nature you were told about. Killing the mountain lions meant the death of many deer and of many trees and bushes. Killing hawks and owls has let mice increase so fast that they do much harm to our crops.

The story of the beaver shows that killing one kind of animal may have far-reaching effects.

Beavers build their homes in ponds. They make ponds by building dams across streams.

There were once many millions of beavers in this country. By building dams they made thousands of ponds. These ponds stored water. They helped to prevent floods. Wild ducks and other wild animals made their homes in and around the ponds.

Beavers have such thick, soft fur that millions were killed. There came to be fewer and fewer beaver dams. There were fewer and fewer homes for other water animals. Water ran into the rivers faster, and floods became more common. The floods carried away good soil and ruined much land. Too late people saw that beavers are important for other things besides fur. The money that has come from beaver skins would not begin to pay for the damage that losing our beaver dams has caused.

Even a few of our diseases can be traced back to the loss of some of our wildlife. Hayfever, for example, is a common disease now. It is caused by the "dust," or pollen, from flowers. The pollen from ragweed causes the most trouble. When most of the land was covered with trees and grass, there were not nearly so many great patches of ragweed as there are now. The ragweed spread when land had its cover of trees and grass taken away and was then let go to waste.

You see, then, that wild plants and animals help you in ways you would never guess.

There is still one more reason why we should try to save our wildlife. Every kind of wildlife really has as much right to live as we have. We are being very selfish as well as very foolish when we say any such thing as, "Let's kill all the hawks because hawks sometimes kill chickens." Haven't the hawks really a right to a part of this land of ours?

Mourning Dove

Trumpeter Swan

What Can We Do?

What can we do to save our wildlife? There are many ways of helping. You could make a list of some of them for yourself.

We can make more of our land into parks and refuges for wildlife. We have helped save the pronghorn just as we did the American bison by giving it special places to live. Refuges set up for it have also helped keep the roseate spoonbill, the bird pictured on the cover, from disappearing.

The trumpeter swan is another big bird we are hoping to save in this way. The trumpeter swan was once one of the wonders of our continent. It is the largest of all our water birds. When these swans flew south in the fall, they flew in great *V*'s, just as wild geese do. But the land around many of the ponds and lakes where they used to live was turned into farms. Besides, hunters killed the swans for their soft feathers. These great birds almost disappeared. Now in two regions where they used to be common there are refuges for them. Laws have been passed, too, to keep them from being killed on their way to the refuges. We may be able to save the trumpeter.

29

Our state parks and our national parks give safe homes to many kinds of wildlife. You are sure to have seen in our parks signs such as "Do not pick wild flowers" and "No hunting allowed at any time." Scattered over many of our states there are small refuges, too. These refuges are very helpful for birds that travel each spring and fall.

The men in charge of our parks understand about balance in nature. They are careful not to upset it. They do not kill off all the meat-eaters to give the game animals a better chance to live.

We can give back to our wild plants and animals some of the homes we have taken away from them. We can turn some of our plowed lands in the West back into grass-lands. We can plant new forests in some places where we have cut forests down. We can let some of our drained marshes become marshes once more.

We can make the water in some of our lakes and rivers fit for fish again. One way is to stop dumping harmful waste materials into the lakes and rivers. Another is to plow our farm land in such a way that not so much mud is washed into streams.

We can be more careful about forest fires than we have been. We should think of every forest fire as ruining the homes of many plants and animals.

We can make laws to keep hunters and fishermen from killing so many of our wild animals. There are already laws protecting many animals. The mourning dove has not disappeared like the passenger pigeon, because laws were made soon enough to protect it.

Our laws should stop the killing of some kinds of wild animals altogether. Hunters and fishermen may be allowed to kill other kinds so long as they do not kill too many.

Pronghorn

But what is too many? Suppose the people of a state want to make a law to protect their deer. They want to keep the number of deer about the same. Then they must not let hunters kill any more grown-up deer in a year than there are baby deer that have a good chance of growing up.

To know how many animals hunters may be allowed to kill, we need to know how many babies different kinds of animals have in a year. We need to know, too, how many of these baby animals will probably live to grow up. Wild animals, you see, have other enemies besides people. Learning about our wild animals helps us save them.

Just having a law does not help any unless people obey it. Laws against killing the bald eagle have not kept it from being killed. Many of our ways of helping save our wildlife cannot be carried on by one person. Our government must carry them on. But obeying laws is something that everyone can do by himself.

Quail, or Bob-white

We can make laws against collecting the eggs of birds that are in danger of disappearing. Stealing an egg is the same thing in the long run as killing a bird.

It is especially hard to protect our birds that go to other countries in their travels. We are getting the help of some of our neighbor countries. We should try to get the help of others.

We are raising some fish and game birds in protected places and are turning them loose. Near a big dam across the Columbia River there is a great fish hatchery that raises young salmon and then turns them into the river. There are many other fish hatcheries. The bob-white is one of the game birds that are being raised and turned loose. Perhaps we could raise more kinds of wildlife than we do.

Many wild animals are killed during hard winters. We can help by feeding them when food is scarce. Of course, we have to know what kinds of food different kinds of animals need.

The story of the big bird in the picture on page 34 shows that what we are doing to save our wildlife is really helping. It will encourage us to do more.

Not long ago some Michigan farmers were surprised to see strange birds flying high above their fields. They were big smoke-colored birds. As they flew, they looked like crosses against the sky.

The farmers had never seen birds like these before. They asked men who study birds about them. They found out that they were sandhill cranes.

Years ago great flocks of sandhill cranes flew over our country, just as did great flocks of whooping cranes and trumpeter swans. The sandhill cranes were called "flying crosses."

The sandhill cranes made their homes in the marshes. Men began draining the marshes to get more farm land. The sandhill cranes lost many of their homes.

Besides, sandhill cranes are good to eat. People shot many of them for food. A sandhill crane lays only two eggs a year. The number of new birds each year did not make up for the ones that were killed.

After a while people saw very few flying crosses. In some parts of the country they were gone altogether.

But in time some of the draining of marshes where the sandhill cranes once lived was stopped. Some of the land became marsh again.

Then the sandhill cranes began to come back to places from which they had been gone for many years. They had safe homes again in the marshes. They could fly from their summer homes to their winter homes without danger of being shot by hunters, for there were now laws to protect them. The baby birds had a good chance to grow up.

There are still not nearly so many sandhill cranes as there once were. But there are more than there were a few years ago. The sandhill cranes have not disappeared.

Laws to protect our wildlife cannot be made once and for all. We must watch to see when changes are needed.

The wood duck is one of our most beautiful wild ducks. More than thirty years ago this duck was put on the list of birds that could not be shot at any time. It was put on the list because it had almost disappeared. Hunters had killed too many.

Simply protecting the wood duck from hunters might not have saved it. But by good luck several people tried raising wood ducks. They were successful. They found that they could hatch the eggs under hens or in incubators. Not so many baby ducks were lost as when the eggs and ducklings were left for the mother duck to take care of. Slowly the number of wood ducks grew.

But as soon as wood ducks began to be more plentiful, hunters began asking to be allowed to kill them again. At last hunters were told that they could kill a very few.

The wood duck still has to be watched carefully. With much killing, it would again be in danger of disappearing. To save it, our government may have to act very quickly. The wood duck might easily become one of the birds your grandchildren will never see.

Sandhill Crane

Wood Duck

Do You Know Now?

1. Some plants and animals that used to be common in our country have now disappeared.

2. Some of the plants and animals we have now are in danger of disappearing.

3. Some of our wild plants and animals are becoming scarce because their homes have been taken away.

4. Many of our wild animals are becoming scarce because there has been too much hunting, trapping, and fishing.

5. In trying to save certain wild animals, we have sometimes done more harm than good.

6. We have cut down our forests so fast that our best forests will soon be gone.

7. Too much picking is killing off our wild flowers.

8. Cutting down a forest or killing off a wild animal may have far-reaching effects.

9. There are many good reasons for trying to save our wildlife.

10. It is not too late to save many of our wild plants and animals. We already know some things we can do.

11. The more we learn about our wild plants and animals, the easier it will be for us to make good plans for keeping them from disappearing.

See for Yourself

1. The heath hen and the Eskimo curlew are two other birds that you will never see. Read their stories in an encyclopedia or in books about birds.

2. There are many other animals besides those you have been told about that are in danger of disappearing. Among them are the manatee, walrus, bighorn mountain sheep, otter, and Alaskan bear. Read in other books about these animals. Try to find out why they are in danger of disappearing.

3. The Fish and Wildlife Service is a part of our national government. It studies our wildlife and plans ways of protecting it. Find out all that you can about the kinds of work it carries on.

4. Visit a fish hatchery if there is one near you.

5. Visit a game farm where game birds are raised.

6. Make a poster that you think will help keep children from picking too many wild flowers.

7. Find out what your state flower is. Is this flower still common in your neighborhood?

8. Probably your state has a conservation committee. If it has, find out from the committee how many wildlife refuges your state has, and where they are.

9. Build a bird-feeding station, and keep it supplied with food during the winter.

10. Find out from other books about the work of the National Audubon Society.

11. Make an S O S map of North America by drawing in, in the regions where they are still found, plants and animals that are in danger of becoming extinct.

12. California condors, like whooping cranes, now number less than 100. Watch in newspapers and magazines for news of these birds.

Litho. in U.S.A